ON A BLADE OF GRASS

LYRICS FROM MY SONGS

LAURIAN TALER

GONG PUBLISHING
TORONTO

By the same author:
Almost Essentials
Under the Blue Sky
So Many Words
Sagacity

ON A BLADE OF GRASS
Lyrics From My Songs
©Laurian Taler, 2014

All rights reserved

Gong Publishing
Toronto

www.gongnog.com

ISBN 978-1-926477-02-2

Laurian Taler

DEDICATION

To all those
who preserved
a romantic bone
over the ages

FOREWORD

This volume continues the publication of the lyrics from my songs started with "Almost Essentials". The title of the volume comes from the title of one of the songs, whose simplicity and directness has attracted me in a number of ways: it has a similarity with the collection of poems by the American poet Walt Whitman, named "Leaves of Grass"; it has a definitely romantic nuance in ringing out the desire and feeling of happiness in a relationship; it goes back to my first nationally published anything, a poem that has been written by me under order for a national children's newspaper when I was not yet 12 years of age. In translation, because it has been written in Romanian, the language in which I had been mainly educated, the first two lines sound like this:

> *In the garden of the palace,*
> *With a blade of grass in my mouth...*

So, you see, I do have a long connection to blades of grass. This connection maybe has influenced in me a certain contemplative view upon things, of which blades of grass, essential to life in their multitude and complex simplicity, have a strong appeal, somehow explaining partially also my higher education as a biologist and biology teacher.

However, as I was trying to explain in the first volume of lyrics, the lines are started almost always after I finish the song and then decide the title for it. The direction of the lyrics, which for me aspire to become poems driven by the song, comes out through that combination between song, title of it, inspiration, and work to make everything palatable, which to me implies a degree of sophistication that respects as much as possible the use of rhythm, rime, and clear meaning within the restrains of the song. It is with these considerations in mind that I believe,

Laurian Taler

as some others do, that lyrics are an important and complex form of poetry, not sufficiently appreciated and sometimes besmirched through the use of flagrant indecency by some promoters of pretended "revolutionary" or radical songs.

A compact disk with the songs from this volume in mp3 format can be purchased separately online from my website www.gongnog.com

On a Blade of Grass

Laurian Taler

TABLE OF CONTENTS

The first two digits beside song title show the CD number,
The last two digits show the position of the song on the CD.

SONG TITLE	PAGE
1005. Only trouble	9
1006. Remember what you said	10
1007. Sing when sun	11
1008. Songs are to sing	12
1009. School start in autumn	13
1010. The meek inherit the earth	14
1301. You'll want to look	15
1302. Amalia's bossa nova	16
1303. Who can taste happiness	17
1304. Throw me a rope	19
1305. Kiss me long	20
1306. I do not believe in angels	21
1307. The dark of early night	22
1308. Hold tight on the ride	23
1309. Long conversations	25
1401. Don't be scared	26
1402. Don't pray for me again	27
1402. Chico from Porto Rico	28
1403. Do not cry my little baby	29
1404. He liked her jogging	30
1405. Who gives me back my child	32
1406. Friendship	33
1407. Make me cry	34
1408. A flower was	35
1409. My first child	37
1410. Tango triste	38
1501. We live in a world	39

1502.	Saturday dreams	40
1503.	So many words	41
1504.	I must ran away	42
1505.	Remember, baby, that I love you	43
1506.	See you just one more time	44
1507.	Listen to your heart	46
1508.	Another day has gone	47
1509.	A long last cry	48
1510.	Fly me down to Italy	49
1701.	Dancing slowly a waltz	50
1702.	What were you thinking	51
1703.	Thank you again	52
1705.	A flower is always a flower	54
1706.	Another fall of the leaves	55
1708.	I long for you so much	56
1709.	Sell me a cow	57
1710.	We can do this my love	58
1802.	A purple blues	59
1803.	Your mind goes further	60
1809.	Don't fly alone	61
1903.	I woke up from a dream	62
1905.	I dream of you	63
1908.	Nostalgia	64
1909.	What is the story	65
1910.	Dreamer	66
2005.	My love for you	67
2006.	Pour some rock	69
2101.	Beam in the dark	70
2102.	Every snow that falls	71
2103.	I sing I'm lonely	72
2104.	On a blade of grass	73
2105.	Remain with me	75
2106.	Snows again	76
2107.	What is after me	77
2108.	You are my love for ever	79
2109.	For thirty years	80

1005. ONLY TROUBLE

Music & lyrics ©2004 Laurian Taler

Intro

What do I do with you
What can I do with you
When I just close my eyes
You jump and torture again my soul

A
You breath only trouble
You provoke to sin
You turned me a rubble
Out of flesh and skin
You are hot and icy
And you make me burn
You are much too spicy
Now I learn

B
Let me go, let me go
Free my mind, free my mind
Be so kind, be so kind
Free my mind, free my mind
Stay away, stay away
From my dreams, from my dreams
Stay away, stay away
Don't send flames, don't send flames
In my soul

   Final
What do I do with you
What can I do with you
When I just close my eyes
You jump and torture again my soul

1006. REMEMBER WHAT YOU SAID

Music & lyrics ©Laurian Taler, 2005

A

Remember what
You said
Remember what
You said

Remember what you said
At our last encounter
I thought that every word
 Comes truly from your heart
But now I see that you
Have done the same as others
Whose words are worth the same,
They cheat and then they maim

B
You said that love
Will ever be
Between us
And that we will share
Ourselves for all our life
That we will grow old together
And discover all the bliss in our souls.

Laurian Taler

1007. SING WHEN SUN

Music & lyrics ©Laurian Taler, 2005

A1
Sing, when everything around you is like spring
Sing, when sun and moon, and stars are all in concert
Sing, with all your heart and all your soul you sing
What is your call for happiness

A2
Sing, when everything around you's summery
Sing, when children have in eyes the spark of heaven
Sing, when flowers and when trees are in their green
Showing with pride their beauty

A3 instrumental

B
Life can be so full, so full of laments
Life can be so full of grumble and groans
It's better to change approach
Get yourself a singing coach
And approach life with a livelier song

A1 (2X)
What's your call for happiness
What's your call for happiness

1008. SONGS ARE TO SING

Music & lyrics ©Laurian Taler, 2005

A
Songs are to sing
What is the beauty in our life
Songs are to sing
What do we feel

Songs are to sing
Where your eyes shine with love
Songs are to sing
How you can smile

Songs are my friends
When I am low and I'm sad
Songs make my heart
Pound with the rhythm

Songs bring the hope
That you will all move like one
Songs pair with you
To make things done.

B
If I cannot sing, I hurt
If I cannot sing, I hurt
Life seems not much more than dirt
Life seems not much more than dirt
(CODA BIS)
If I cannot sing, I hurt
So much.

Laurian Taler

1009. SCHOOL STARTS IN AUTUMN

Music & lyrics ©Laurian Taler, 2008

A
School starts in autumn
School starts in autumn
I'm so excited
That I can't explain
Meeting new people
And learning a fortune
And rubbing a frenzy of thoughts

B
I decided that my road in life
Goes through knowing what I need to know
To be able to build what I want
Make a marking future for all my world

C1,
I'll learn how to grow most flowers
I'll learn where to find energy
I'll design
What never was
I'll invent
Better worlds

C2
I'll learn how to deal with brethren
I'll learn how to juggle heavy tasks
I'll spread love that will well thrive
I'll stir up sanity
I'll stir up sanity

1010. THE MEEK INHERIT THE EARTH

Music & lyrics ©Laurian Taler, 2005

A
The meek inherit the earth
They save it from certain death
With care and with so much love
Forests they plant, and work the soil

B
The meek inherit the earth
They save it from certain death
With care and so much love
With their brains and with their will

C
You have the brains and the power
You must do what's in your power
You have the brains and the power
You must do what's in your power

A, B

D
Do your part, do your part
And save the earth
Do your part, do your part
And save the earth

1301. YOU'LL WANT TO LOOK

Music & lyrics ©Laurian Taler, 2006

A1
You'll want to look very careful around
You'll want to hear the smallest of sounds
You'll want to be on alert every blink
You'll want to know what your neighbour may think
If water becomes scarce

A2
You'll want to have your dear own mask
You'll want to know how to breath from a flask
You'll want to crawl for a tank of fresh air
You'll want to kill for some air to spare
If air becomes so scarce

B
What are you doing now
Reuse, reduce, recycle the world
What are you doing now
Don't wait for the world to go bad

B, B

A3
You'll want to look very careful around
You'll want to be on the top of the mound
You'll want to grab and to hold every crumb
You'll want to eat even pit of a plum
If all food becomes scarce

A2, B, B,

1302. AMALIA'S BOSSA NOVA

Music & lyrics ©Laurian Taler, 2006

Amalia loves a slow bossa nova
Cause she dances only slow bossa nova
She dances with passion with her own lov'ah
But then she goes home
And sleeps in her own bed

Amalia thinks as straight as an arrow
She wants to be the wife of a pharaoh
Or maybe get hold of a tycoon
And bear him a baby with a silver spoon

For this purpose some may tremble a lot
But Amalia knows that she is so hot
Any man who only glances at her
Has his heart so burned forever

Question is why are the pharaohs so few
And where are these tycoons hiding from view
Is there anyone around at the ball
Will he dance with her at all

Amalia loves a slow bossa nova
Cause she dances only slow bossa nova
She dances with passion with her own lov'ah
But then she goes home
And sleeps in her own bed

Amalia thinks as straight as an arrow
She wants to be the wife of a pharaoh
Or maybe get hold of a tycoon
And bear him a baby with a silver spoon
And bear him a baby with a silver spoon
And bear him a baby with a silver spoon

1303. WHO CAN TASTE HAPPINESS

Music & lyrics ©Laurian Taler, 2006

Who can taste happiness
With this global progress
In which you have no time
For your lover

You get emails all day
And you push text away
While your cell phone's a buzz
Every moment

You must work twenty-four
You must work until sore
And commuting's a bore
And takes time.

Who can taste happiness
When the planet's a mess
In which man is to man
Adversary

Who can taste happiness
If more people have less
Than to keep them alive
For a fortnight

On a Blade of Grass

Life's expendable for
Those who sell arms and gore
With a commerce that runs
Billions

When to flourish we could
Make peace ever, bring food
To the hungry and should
Spread the love

Who can taste happiness
When the planet's a mess
In which man is to man
Adversary

Who can taste happiness
If more people have less
Than to keep them alive
For a fortnight

When to flourish we could
Make peace ever, bring food
To the hungry and should
Spread the love

1304. THROW ME A ROPE

Music & lyrics ©Laurian Taler, 2006

A1
Throw me a rope
'Cause you can save me
Throw me a rope
And pull me out
If you believe that I deserve it
Throw me a rope and save me now
Throw me a rope and save me now
Throw me a rope and save me now

A2
Throw me a rope
I know you loved me
Maybe you still
Feel love for me
In desperation I have fallen
So low I can't climb out alone
So low I can't climb out alone
So low I can't climb out alone

B 1
Life's been good for you
When we were holding hands
Life's been good for you
When I was up

B 2 (2x)
You were radiant
And extravagant
And the world turned
Around you for me

A1

1305. KISS ME LONG

Music & lyrics ©Laurian Taler, 2006

A (2x)
Kiss me long
I long for you
Even when
You're in my arms
Kiss me long
I long for you
I'm more thirsty
Of your charms

B
Your gentle touch comes from heaven
Your lips are balm for my heart
There is no taste in the world that compares
The tang of your mouth on mine

Kiss me long
I long for you
Even when
You're in my arms
Kiss me long
I long for you
I'm more thirsty
Of your charms

Kiss me long, Kiss me long
Kiss me long, Kiss me long
Kiss me long, Kiss me long

1306. I DO NOT BELIEVE IN ANGELS

Music & lyrics ©Laurian Taler, 2006

I do not believe in angels
I do not believe in devils
I do not believe in magic
I do not believe in bad spells

I only believe
That you are a thief
That you stole my mind
And you stole my heart

I only believe
That you are a thief
That you stole my mind
And you stole my heart

B
How will I get my heart back
And my mind that's off the rack
Maybe you'd give me a clue
Or I'd have to sing in your face
How much I love you

Or I'd have to sing in your face
How much I love you
Or I'd have to sing in your face
How much I love you

1307. THE DARK OF EARLY NIGHT

Music & lyrics ©Laurian Taler, 2005

A1
The dark of early night
Gives me a frosty fright
It's not the lack of light
But void of loneliness
The time stretches the void
And I become annoyed
There's nothing I could fill
With all this emptiness.

It's darker in my heart
Than anywhere you think
And colder it is too
I freeze my mind to it
As I am still alone
Since you have left my soul
And raped my only hope
For tender happiness

c
 Whatever's in your heart right now
You must know how you hurt a man
And maybe you can feel restraint
So not to hurt again

I do not wish another one
To suffer what I feel
Suffer what I feel
Suffer what I feel
Suffer what I feel

1308. HOLD TIGHT ON THE RIDE

Music & lyrics ©Laurian Taler, 2005

A1
Hold tight on the ride
It's up and down
Hold tight on the ride
It's like a tide
Hold tight on the ride
You cannot hide
Bring out your emotions
Or you'll die
A2
Hold tight on the ride
I am your guide
Hold tight on the ride
Don't eat your pride
Hold tight on the ride
The turns are wide
Bring out your emotions
Be a clown
B1
Life is us riding together,
In the unknown of mankind
No matter if a stormy weather
Tries to give us a hard time
B2
Life is us riding so together,
Eyes to eyes and hand in hand
With blue skies or stormy weather
Our love's a magic wand

A1
C
Everybody goes through life on waves
Rowing up and down

On a Blade of Grass

Everybody goes through life on waves
On tides
Hard as your life is
You keep afloat
With your head
Up, up in the sun
Eyes burning

A1

B1
Life is us riding together,
In the unknown of mankind
No matter if a stormy weather
Tries to give us a hard time

B3
Life is us riding together, together
Eyes to eyes and hand in hand
With blue skies or stormy weather
Our love's a magic wand
Our great love (3x)

Laurian Taler

1309 LONG CONVERSATIONS

Music & lyrics ©Laurian Taler, 2006

A1
Long conversations about love
About the future, about the world
We had forever, day and night
Hoping to grow good with our might

A2
They made our hair turn all white
Over years teaching kids
Long conversations about love
About good, about folks
About us

B1
Even the long pauses
When we kept quiet
Were full of meaning
And heavy with love
My eyes were searching
For the warmth of your eyes
And they were filling with
Tears of joy

B2

A1, A1, A2

1310. DON'T BE SCARED

Music & lyrics ©Laurian Taler, 2006

A
Don't be scared I'm beside you everywhere
Don't be scared I am guarding here and there

Don't be scared I'll be with you all the way
Don't be scared I'll be with you night and day

Don't be scared I'll take care when you need
Don't be scared I'll take care when you need

B
You are all for me
You are all my reasons
You are all for me
You are heaven and earth
I'll look after you and hold you close my dear
I'll look after you wherever you are
Yes where you are

Laurian Taler

1401. DON'T PRAY FOR ME AGAIN

Music & lyrics ©Laurian Taler, 2006

A1
Don't pray for me again
After I've got you this hell of a pain
Don't pray for me
I don't deserve
Your deepest thoughts
After my acts

A2
 Don't pray for me again
You can only forget so much in love
I am not worth the torment that I made
With my ways breaking your heart

B
You deserve to live
The best of life
With another mate
You deserve to live
The best of life
Without me in your sight
It was the same lack of luck
A drake chasing for a duck
And the duck enamoured
Falling such an easy prey

1402. CHICO FROM PORTO RICO

Music & lyrics ©Laurian Taler, 2005

Chico from Porto Rico
Chico has gone downtown
Chico from Porto Rico
Chico has put roots down

Chico from Porto Rico
Has found there a sweet girl
Chico from Porto Rico
Calls her his dearest pearl

But his Chica wanted to impression
When she walks along with him downtown
So, she asked him, "Dear caballero,
Buy me right away the newest gown."
(bis)

Chico from Porto Rico
Bought her a fancy dress
Chico from Porto Rico
Is now in bigger mess

Chico from Porto Rico
Must buy her now a ring
As Chica wants to marry
She won't accept a fling

How will Chico get out of this trouble
You imagine, as you might do same
Don't be shy, but don't be neither rubble,
Learn to live well but without blame. (bis)

1403. DO NOT CRY MY LITTLE BABY

Music & lyrics ©Laurian Taler, 2001

A1
Do not cry my little baby
Do not cry my sweetest soul
Do not cry my little baby
Better play with me your role

A2
Do not cry my little baby
You'll grow up to laugh in life
Do not cry my little baby
Your enjoyment will be rife

B (2x)
You'll have fun and jest
And pleasure
And from agony you'll fly
You don't need to cry,
Don't need to cry
You'll see you'll have the best

A1, A

1404. HE LIKED HER JOGGING

Music & lyrics ©Laurian Taler, 2006

A1
He liked her jogging,
She ran always with a smile
It made him happy
And ran after her a while
But couldn't reach her
'Cause she was so strong and fast
And he was sluggish like a log
And knew his running wouldn't last

B1 (HE)
Wait for me, my dear jogger,
My legs are those of a blogger
I will start to exercise
To get stronger in my thighs
For your legs and for your smile
I'll run again another mile
I'll run again another mile
I'll run again another mile
I'll catch you soon
I'll catch you soon
I'll catch you soon

A2
She saw him trudging
Like a tug-boat in distress
She knew he wanted her
In a state of undress
Because his cuteness
She would not say no at all
But neither would she say a yes
Without him giving her a call

B2 (SHE)
Exercise, my dear blogger,
If you want to be a jogger
And you want to catch me still
Keep on using the treadmill
When you're sure you won't stall
Pump up your heart, give me a call
Pump up your heart, give me a call
Pump up your heart, give me a call
Or else get lost
Or else get lost
Or else get lost

B3
HE: I am pumping up my heart
And whatever other part
To run with you at your rate
And become your jogging mate
SHE: You become my jogging mate
If for our lives you are my date
If for our lives you are my date
If for our lives you are my date
BOTH:
You are my date
You are my date
You are my date

1405. WHO GIVES ME BACK MY CHILD

Music & lyrics © Laurian Taler, 2004

A1
Who gives me back my child
That fell in your bad war
Who gives me back my child
His laughter is no more
Who gives me back my child
Tears are running wild
Who gives me back my child
Despair I cannot roar

B
Life is not to see
Children not to be
Life is not to taste
Children as some waste
Only I now stand
And can't understand
Why is life unfair
With so much despair

C
A world where people die too young
And parents are left just to mourn
No matter how just is the fighting
Their heart is just ripped- for their born
A world where people are killing
The hopes of the young and the old
Is no world to live in,
Make the world anew!

1406. FRIENDSHIP

Music & lyrics ©Laurian Taler, 2000

You call me friend
I call you friend
We are both liars
What's between us
So much fracas
Is something else (bis)

You put me down
I put you down
We are both downers
To go like this
Doesn't make sense
For none of us at all

But,
Friendship
Whatever its name
Is what we want
Friendship
With all its meaning
Is what we want
Friendship
Be fight or quarrel
Is what we want
As when we
Were children
And truly friends
(bis)

1407. MAKE ME CRY

Music & lyrics ©Laurian Taler, 2005

A
Make me cry, make me smile, I'm deluded
That you'll know how to bring me the bliss
But as so many times
You confuse me with rhymes
And you bring me the usual pain

But as so many times
You confuse me with rhymes
And you bring me the usual pain

B
You say you'll change,
That you will care
But all these lies
I cannot bear
I made my mind, yes,
You aren't my kind
A truthful soul
I will find.

A

1408. A FLOWER WAS

Music & lyrics © Laurian Taler, 2001

A1
A flower was,
A flower stayed
It was her name
With eyes so large
With smile so strange
It made her fame

2x
Her hair like a river
Her looks made you shiver
Mysterious silence
Surrounded her presence
And made you believe in gods

B
My goddess she
Might have become
If she had tried
To share with me
All her so deep
Dark serenity
But she had turned her eyes
To other flame
And thrown then were the dice
To the love game
A flower wilted pain
In me

A2
What happened next
I do not know
As I have left

On a Blade of Grass

The soil that grew
The flower who
Made me bereft
(2x)
But deep in my glimmers
Her strange smile still simmers
I crave for that flower
Each night and each hour
And hope she met happiness

C
The story has a happy end
My heart I soon could gracefully mend
And out of a wild encompassing love
A new flower sprung

We called her Fleur for all the blooms
That beauty in all our lives bring
The beauty that keeps again flourishing
The eternal spring

Laurian Taler

1409. MY FIRST CHILD (TO XENIA)

Music and lyrics ©Laurian Taler, 2000

1
My first child is having her
Very own child soon
My first child, my first light,
And my hope for the moon
She'll become a mother like her mother, my love
Tender and kind
Serene and happy
Love of my soul

2
Years have gone, and friends have gone
Yet something remained
All the bliss to see you grow
And mother your child
Child your mother was before we kindled our love
Love that is you
Life now you give
Love blossomed in you

Choir
Your mother's love, your sister's love
Your husband's love for family
Your father's love and your own love
Are all above serenity
You have the link to all eternity
You have the link to soul
Another soul you'll grow and she
Will empower and make whole

1410. TANGO TRISTE

Music & lyrics ©Laurian Taler, 2008

A1
A sad and slow tango
Curls around my lone soul
A sad and slow tango
Finds its way in my bowl
A sad and slow tango
Oppresses my thoughts so

B
Doesn't matter whom I have in my arms dancing
Doesn't matter if she is a fair dancer
Doesn't matter if she laughs or cries with me
If it's not you I embrace, it's a sad tango

A2
A sad and slow tango
It's all what I deserve
A sad and slow tango
Is getting on my nerves
A sad and slow tango
Leaves me without the verve

1501. WE LIVE IN A WORLD (BALD JAZZ)

Music & lyrics ©Laurian Taler, 2002

A
We live in a world full of surprise
No matter we are stupid or wise
We cannot see what comes next
And most perplexed
Act but good not realize

We live in a world full of misfits
No matter we are with or no wits
We do not find how to cope
And shooting dope
Fail our limits to admit
Bis

B
 Look here, traveller
 You can't be reveller
 Put forces together Heather
And build the bridge that binds
'Cause you can't stay long
On doing wrong
Forever, Forever

A
C
Come bond with your fellow
Soul of mankind
Come bond with your fellow
Do good, do mind
Come bond with your fellow
Build future now
Come bond with your fellow
Sing for it now
Bis C

1502. SATURDAY DREAMS

Music & lyrics ©Laurian Taler, 2007, 2009

A1
I woke up on a Saturday
With fragments of some dreams
They circled vaguely in my mind
Trying to settle down
They got more furious in their swirl
And became much more dense
I kept connecting piece by piece
All started to make sense
B
We live in this world to grow with hope
That our efforts, up a slope
Roll down towards peace
Peace that brings all what we need
To share bliss
A2 (2x)
Stretch your hands and clasp someone
Making common front
Doing good for all mankind
With open heart
C
 It might sound vague
'Cause it's a dream
But without our dreams we cannot hope
To overcome the fights that kill
And turn mankind in war mill
Let's wake up, it is not too late
And turn up our dreams in love, not hate
In hugging a good cause that saves
Mankind from return to caves

(Repeat from A, tempo 160)

1503. SO MANY WORDS

Music & lyrics ©Laurian Taler, 2006

A1
So many words I have learned
Just to describe
The beauty in hidden things
The beauty in stones and skies
But no words are for your eyes

A2
So many words I have learned
To whisper sweet
In willing ears, amazed,
Enchanted, full of delight,
Forging charming dreams,
But no words come at your sight

B
Dazzling, you turn heads
Without an effort,
Glamour at its best,
Nature full of zest,
Flash never amiss
Your person inspire bliss

A1, A2

1504. I MUST RUN AWAY

Music & lyrics ©Laurian Taler, 2006

I must run away
From all the lies I lied
From all the pain I caused to you
From all the guilt I've got
From all the words that hurt
From all the nights you sobbed for me
From all the nights we missed

I must run away
From all the lies I lied
From all the pain I caused to you
From all the guilt I've got
From all the words that hurt
From all the nights you sobbed for me
From all the nights we missed

From all the nights you sobbed for me
From all the nights we missed

I must then come back again
Burning to rebuild your new happiness
Ready to renew our grace
As spring always renews
All the world

I must then come back to you
Cause you are my eternal flame

1505. REMEMBER, BABY

Music & lyrics ©Laurian Taler, 2006

Remember, baby, that I love you
Remember, baby, that I love you
There is nothing else that needs now to be said
There is nothing else that you need to feel true
If you can remember all the nights and all the days
That we filled with hot love, with real love, going both ways
Then you can forgive me one more time

Remember, baby, that I love you
Remember, baby, that I love you, oh, so much
Our history together
Is a seal that we cannot break
We will stay happy together
With our love
With our love
With our love

People make mistakes'cause they love and forget
People make mistakes when so heavy they bet
If one lets oneself caught in a pool of sin for a while
Then it's easy to end
Without love

Remember, baby, that I love you
Remember, baby, that I love you ,oh so much
Our history together
Is a seal that we cannot break
We will stay happy together
With our love
With our love
With our love

1506. SEE YOU JUST ONE MORE TIME

Music & lyrics ©Laurian Taler, 2006

See you just
One more time
I want to hug you just
One more time
Maybe you'll open your heart
Love at first sight ain't true

See you just
One more time
I want to hug you just
One more time
Maybe you'll open your cold heart
Love at first sight ain't true

One more time
One more time
One more time

Since I saw you for the first time
Everything seems to taste like lime
I do not understand all my pain
I sleep with your face behind my eyelids

Since I saw you for the first time
Everything seems to taste like lime
I do not understand all my pain
I sleep with your face behind my eyelids

See you just
One more time
I want to hug you just
One more time
Maybe you'll open your heart

Laurian Taler

Love at first sight ain't true

See you just
One more time
I want to hug you just
One more time
Maybe you'll open your cold heart
Love at first sight ain't true

One more time
One more time
One more time

Now there is no doubt in my mind
I must see you or I'll become blind
Blind to what has been beauty before
I have to see you once more (3x)

1507. LISTEN TO YOUR HEART

Music and lyrics ©Laurian Taler, 2006

A
Listen to your heart
It lets you know so many things
Listen to your heart
It puts you breaks or give you wings
It tells you all
Listen to your heart
It's pumping you with energy
So that life gets full
And you enjoy it mightily (2x)

B
Listen to your heart
It murmurs softly in your chest
Listen to your heart
It tells you how to be your best
Listen to your heart
It thumps and thumps for all your life
Keeping you in shape, yes,
Make it work harder for your part
Give it a work out, it's your heart

C (2x)
Listen
It tells you a story about love
Listen
It makes you know when your love arrived
It gives you worries
Makes you fill flurries
Lets you have scurries
Listen to your heart

1508. ANOTHER DAY HAS GONE

Music & lyrics ©Laurian Taler, 2006

A
Another day has gone
Another night has gone
I can't say that I suffer
Since you have gone away
Why say what isn't true
I'll manage without you
The world isn't just fools
 A good heart I will find
To go by better rules -
And be kind

B
Another day will go without you
I feel so liberated now
Another night will go without you
Without the torments and the row
I'll build without you my own future
You will rule me no more
Life will become what I will want it to be

C
Another day has gone, has gone away
Another day has gone away
Another day has gone away
Another day has gone away

A

1509. A LONG LAST CRY

Music & lyrics ©Laurian Taler, 2006

A
Let me have at least as good-bye
A long last cry
I won't be for you a necktie
A long last cry

B (2x)
You have made me cry so often
Not a teardrop could soften
What became a surly, stony
And dry heart,
And dry heart

C (2x)
I don't cry because I lose you
I don't need a choke of grief
I just want to cleanse my spirit
With relief
With relief
(Second time)
With relief

A, B

1510. FLY ME DOWN TO ITALY

Music & lyrics ©Laurian Taler, 2006, 2008

A
Fly me down to Italy
Where sky and sea encounter
Fly me down to Italy
And let your love flow to me
My love flows to you
Fly me down to Italy
Where song and wine are friendly
Fly me down to Italy
And caress the soul in me

B
There I will be free
Like a new baby's glance
And I'll caress your hair
And keep you in a trance
I'll share with you
All the depths of me
I'll sing you crazy songs
For happiness

A, B, A

1701. DANCING SLOWLY

Music & lyrics ©Laurian Taler, 2006

A1
Dancing slowly a waltz
With you, love, in my arms
It returns those old feelings in me
Dancing slowly a waltz
With you, love, in my arms
Is re-falling in love with you

A2
Dancing slowly a waltz
With you, love, in my arms
For a century, even for more
Dancing slowly a waltz
With you, love, in my arms
Is our life with our love at its core

B1
Mountains we climbed
And some valleys went down
Some days were greyer
And some nights seemed brown

C (2x)
But we stayed together
Foreheads up in the weather
And built for happiness our nest

A2

Laurian Taler

1702. WHAT WERE YOU THINKING

Music & lyrics ©Laurian Taler, 2007

A1
What were you thinking
You want to ruin my life
What were you thinking
I don't need again this strife
What were you thinking
What were you thinking
What were you thinking
I will never be your doll

A2
What were you thinking
You think I'll do what you say
What were you thinking
To take me down in the hay
What were you thinking
What were you thinking
What were you thinking
For your rotten act you'll pay

B1
I am a person like you
I have dreams and life plans too
You want to take just advantage of me
To have your fun then leave

B2
If you would have wanted love
You should have shown me your love
Not just a moment of desire spent
For this you'll sure repent

A1, A2

1703. THANK YOU AGAIN

Music & lyrics ©Laurian Taler, 2007

A1
Thank you again
For all the happiness
Thank you again
For all the zaniness
Thank you again
For being what you are
Thank you again
For being without par
My love

B
Whenever times were
For us harder
Whenever something wrong
Came between us
You knew how to bring peace
Under our roof
With your noblesse
And largesse
Your limitless
Earthiness
And heartily
Homeliness
For love

A2
Thank you again
For all the bitterness
That you have shared
With me nevertheless
Thank you again
For all the patience

Laurian Taler

Thank you again
For your resilience
My love

A1
Thank you again
For all the happiness
Thank you again
For all the zaniness
Thank you again
For being what you are
Thank you again
For being without par
My love

B

1705. A FLOWER IS ALWAYS A FLOWER

Music & lyrics ©Laurian Taler, 2007

A1
A flower is always a flower
If open or if just a bud
A flower is always a flower
If it's a lassie for a lad

A2
A flower is always a flower
No matter if it's red or green
A flower is always a flower
If love with it is what you mean

B1 (2x)
A bunch if you give
Or one receive
What matter the most
Is their host
A flower can be
To heart the key
Send your sign
Of "Please be mine"
Or just "I am your friend"

A1, A2 (last line 3x)

1706. ANOTHER FALL OF THE LEAVES

Music & lyrics ©Laurian Taler, 2006

A1
Another fall of the leaves
Turns me again nostalgic
Another fall of the leaves
Brings autumn in my heart

A2
Another fall of the leaves
On hills and on the alleys
Reminds me of my own love
Of its mountains and valleys

A1, A2

B (2x)
Another fall of the leaves
All the regrets I discard now
I renew will in my soul
Full of love
To climb the mountains with you

A1, A2

1708. I LONG FOR YOU SO MUCH

Music & lyrics ©Laurian Taler, 2007

A1
I long for you so much,
For your eyes, for your touch,
For what you make me feel
For the life you'n me instil

A2
I long for you again,
Our hearts to enchain
Together in a kiss
Reach again our bliss.

B
If you are away
I feel alone
Even if I know
That you will return
Always full of love

If you are with me
I feel reborn
With new strengths to tie
Our hearts for life
Always full of love

A1, A2

1709. SELL ME A COW

Music & lyrics ©Laurian Taler, 2006

A1
Sell me a cow
And a piece of land
Where the green meets the end
I'd grow the cow into a heard of calves
And milk to market I'd send

A2
I'd ride a horse
On this piece of land
I'd do some horsing around
But soon I'd find me a wife to love
And put some strong roots to ground

B1
And with some help from good neighbours
And with twenty hours labour
I would build my wife a palace
To keep her away from malice
And enlarge our lovely family

B2
And with some help from good neighbours
And with twenty hours labour
I would build my wife a palace
To keep her away from malice
And enlarge our family

1710. WE CAN DO THIS, MY LOVE

Music & lyrics ©Laurian Taler, 2007

A1
We can do this, my love
We can do this
It's only our will that counts
We can do this, my love
We can do this
It's our life that's paramount

B1
We can do this, my love
We can do this
We can't forbid our love to grow
We can do this, my love
We can do this
In our eyes our love must glow

A2
Don't be afraid, my love
Don't be afraid
Together for all we'll be brave
Don't be afraid, my love
Don't be afraid
We'll float together on life's wave

B2
We can do good, my love
We can do good
In truth and goodness we can rise
We can do good, my love
We can do good
In truth and goodness we'll be wise

1802. A PURPLE BLUES

Music & lyrics ©Laurian Taler, 2006

A1
A purple blues, I sing a purple blues
A purple blues, it is my only muse

A2 (2x)
I sing it when I'm sad
I sing it when I'm mad
I sing it when I feel
Entire world is turning harsher against me

B1
Purple blues
You are my safety valve
Purple blues
You cut all my stress right in half

B2
Purple blues
Purple blues
My muse and saviour
What I'd do without you
I do not know

A1

A2 (final)
I sing it when I'm sad
I sing it when I'm mad
I sing it when I feel
World is turning against me
World is turning against me
World is turning against me
Purple blues, oh, purple blues

1803. YOUR MIND GOES FURTHER

Music and lyrics ©Laurian Taler, 2006

Dedicated to my friend Vova

Your mind goes further
Than any car
Your mind goes further
Keep it ajar

Your mind goes further
Than any plane
Just make it pry bars
And keep it sane

From the smallest of smallness
To the largest of great
Your thoughts can wander
Against whatever fate

From the wonder of flowers
And the sunrise awake
Your thoughts have power
Any strange shape to take

Your mind goes further
In time and space
Your mind goes further
No matter the race

Your mind goes further
The truths to find
And spread them with care
To another mind

1809. DON'T FLY ALONE

Music & lyrics ©Laurian Taler, 2007

A1
Don't fly alone
Because the sky is too large
Don't run alone
Because the earth is so wide
Don't walk alone
As roads are too long for one
Don't be alone
Find one to go
With you

A2
Don't fly alone
Because the sky is too blue
Don't run alone
Because the earth is so green
Don't walk alone
As roads are too grey for one
Keep the hopes up high
Because
Someone will
Someone will
Join you soon

B
Life is a road where you need good company
Life is a run to best share with somebody
Life is a flight in the sky highs and the lows
Don't fly your life ever alone

A1, A2

1903. I WOKE UP FROM A DREAM

Music & lyrics ©Laurian Taler, 2007, 2011

A1
I woke up from a dream
Imagines rather dim
Were turning in my head
It was some good, some bad
About you I felt sad

A2
You travelled on a train
From mountains to a plain
With someone I don't know
He seemed to me a foe
He seemed to be your beau

B1
But then I saw you sleeping tight
In our bed and I felt right
Bad dream, go fast away
Oh, what a happy feeling
To know that we are safe
Oh, what a happy feeling
To know that we are safe

B2
To wake up from whatever dream
And be together is supreme
I'd fight with all the foes
Oh, what a happy feeling
To know that we are safe
Oh, what a happy feeling
To know that we are safe

Laurian Taler

1905. I DREAM OF YOU

Music & lyrics ©Laurian Taler, 2007

I dream of you
Of you alone
Night after night
I dream of you

I dream of you
Hoping the night
Does never end
I dream of you

But all mornings return
And with them the dreams all go
In place descends the great sadness
Like a grey shroud it will cover
My view of things and my hopes regarding you
Shroud disappear from my view

In the light of the day
Sometimes dreams so seem to melt
But the dream of you
Stays with me deep in my heart

1908. NOSTALGIA

Music & lyrics ©Laurian Taler, 2006

A1
Nostalgia, Nostalgia
What you make of me
I am longing
Of that happy past

A2
Nostalgia, Nostalgia
Keep away from me
Too much sadness
In my heart you cast

B
Grieving on shadows gone
May turn black any weak heart
Better to break the spell
Nostalgia, you better go to hell

A3
Nostalgia, Nostalgia
I feel free from you
I no longer
Leave in ancient past

A4
Nostalgia, Nostalgia
No regrets are due
I am leaving
Sorrow in the dust

A1, A2, B

Laurian Taler

1909. WHAT IS THE STORY

Music & lyrics ©Laurian Taler, 2007

A1
I don't know yet
What is the story
Between you, between me
And our love
But I know now
That there is something
That we are
Both moved hard in our heart

B
What I feel
You should feel in your heart
What you feel
I must feel in my own heart
Is it so or it is
Something else
But I know
People would say
That this is love

A2
I think I know
What is the story
Between you, between me
And our love
A man has found
His rightful pair
A woman has just found
Her own man

B, A2

1910. DREAMER

Music and words ©Laurian Taler, 2004

A dreamer I was born
And a dreamer I will stay
Till my midnight
My soul is filled with dreams
And my eyes are seeing things
Closed or open

Tortured by life
Escape in night
Without borders
Without orders

I am just what I dream
And I dream of seraphim
That I'll make with you
Tonight

2
No matter how hard it will be
I'll make this dream alive, you'll see,
We'll build our future,
We'll build our future,
We'll start our future
Tonight
(bis)

Laurian Taler

2005. MY LOVE FOR YOU

Music & lyrics ©Laurian Taler, 2007

A1
My love for you
Doesn't have bounds
My love for you
Flies over mounds
My love for you
Trembles in night

My love for you
Grows at your sight
My love for you
Keeps my heart right

A2
Your love for me
Is elixir
Your love for me
Is so sincere
Your love for me
My songs inspire

Your love for me
Gives me the fire
Your love for me
Gives me the fire
To love you
To love you
To love you
To love you

B1
In the wilderness of life
You are my only refuge

On a Blade of Grass

Friend and lover, and then wife

With me till the last deluge
With me till the last deluge
Beautifying wherever you walk
Make me get over any roadblock
You inspire
My desire

And you fill
My dream empire
With all your love
With all your love
With all your love

A2

2006. POUR SOME ROCK

Music & lyrics ©Laurian Taler, 2008

A1
Pour some rock in my blood, love (/ boy / girl)
Get the gig grooving good
(As good as you groove)
Pour some rock in my blood, love (/ boy / girl)
Shoot me high into mood
(As high as you could)

B
Rock goes down, goes down to my soul
Soul goes up, goes up to my goal
Goal I reach, I reach like a ball
Rock's the one that started it all

A2
When I rock I'm with you, love (/ boy / girl)
When I rock I'm on cue, love (/ boy / girl)
When I rock I'm your fool, love (/ boy / girl)
I'm your fool for the night

A3
When I rock I'm with you, love (/ boy / girl)
When I rock I'm on cue, love (/ boy / girl)
When I rock I'm your fool, love (/ boy / girl)
Rock me gently and tight

2101. BEAM IN THE DARK

Music & lyrics ©Laurian Taler, 2005

A
Beam in the dark of life
You are to my soul
Beam in the dark of life
To my soul
You are
You shine for me
A path to take
And to hold
A starry guide
To me you are

B (2x)
Shine on me
With your bright light
Till the end
Bring me warmth
Bring me sweetest
Candour

Keep the fire up
In your heart
Melt desires that
I might have
Boiling down in my dark
Secret space

C =B (instrumental)

2102. EVERY SNOW THAT FALLS

Music & lyrics ©Laurian Taler, 2005

A1
Every snow that falls
Reminds me of your magic
Every snow that falls
Reminds me of your smile
A2
Every snow that falls
Reminds me of our sheer madness
When we wanted in spite of all
Fly to moon, yes, fly to moon

B1
I'd fly to the moon
With you every night
With clouds of snow in the background
With stars and your angel smile
B2
I'd fly to the moon
With you every night and day
Holding you tender in my arms
And singing to you a song with stars

A1
Every snow that falls
Reminds me of your magic
Every snow that falls
Reminds me of your smile
A2
Every snow that falls
Reminds me of our sheer madness
When we wanted in spite of all
Fly to moon, yes, fly to moon

2103. I SING I'M LONELY

Music & lyrics ©Laurian Taler, 2005

A
I sing,
I sing I'm lonely
Because you left me
Because you didn't want to
Share happiness
With me
I sing I'm lonely
Because you left me
Because you were so selfish
Wanting to take all
All my heart
All my heart
All my heart

B
If you were to share
We could be a pair
If you were to stay
We could've gone
All the way
Maybe it's still time
To return and to be mine
Maybe it's still time
To return and to be mine

A

2104. ON A BLADE

Music & lyrics ©Laurian Taler, 2011

A1
On a blade
On a blade
On a blade of grass
There was a little bird
And that bird
And that bird
And that bird
Gave me a sense of happiness

A2
Happiness
Happiness
Happiness
Is such a complicated word
I don't know
Why a bird
On a blade of grass
Can make such a charade

B
I guess it 's cause I saw you smile
Once in a field
The sky was just as blue
As your enchanting eyes
You were caressing grass
And you were singing softly like a bird

C1
I was happy
I was so happy
How little we need
To be happy

On a Blade of Grass

How little we need
To be happy

C2
I was happy
I was so happy
 How little we need
A blade of grass,
A smile, a blue sky
And a song from you

A1, A2

2105. REMAIN WITH ME

Music & lyrics ©Laurian Taler, 2005

A1
Remain with me
Remain with me
This night must end with you beside
Remain with me
Remain with me
The day that comes will nothing hide

A2
I am a fool
I am a fool
I cannot live without your touch
I am a fool
I am a fool
If it's not love I don't know much

B1
Lean on me for all your troubles
Lean on me for good
Lean on me if you feel weaker
Or you change your mood
Lean on me a minute
Lean on me a life
Hand in hand
For happiness or strife

A1, A2
Finale

2106. SNOWS AGAIN

Music & lyrics ©Laurian Taler, 2005

A
Snows again
Like it has snowed
When we first met,
My love
It was cold
But you were hot
And I got burnt
By love
You smiled like
A million suns
My heart pumped
Blood like a gun
And the music
Played for us
A slow tango

B
Snow was everywhere
Around us falling
It was our magic moment that bonds
From then on we knew that we were two in one
Many snows and summers kept us one

A2
Snows again
Snows again
Snows again

2107. WHAT IS AFTER ME

Music & lyrics ©Laurian Taler, 2005

A1
What was before me
What is after me
Where is my future
How I change the world
To better mankind
Make a better future

B1
Million questions jump
Asking my brain
What's going to happen?
Do I have to choose
Or I have to let
Whatever will be?

I have to do
A lot of things
To make life shine

A1, B1

A2
Who created time
Who created space
Who created planets
How did matter move
From a ball of mud
To make me a thinker

B2
How we better learn
Keep life alive

On a Blade of Grass

Harmony with nature
How we help ourselves
To spread happiness
To the entire world

I have to do
A lot of things
To make life shine

2108. YOU ARE MY LOVE FOREVER

Music & lyrics ©Laurian Taler, 2005, 2008

A1
You are my love forever
Forever is for you and me
Even if forever is such a big word
Forever all my love will be

A2
With you time disappears
With you I know that I live
From the small sounds
From beatings of my heart
Heart that beats only to love you

B
Earthquakes or eruptions
Of the volcanoes
Ain't enough to stop
My love for you
Revolutions, riots
Or even famine
Ain't enough to little
What I feel

A1, B, A2

On a Blade of Grass

2109. FOR THIRTY YEARS

Music and lyrics ©Laurian Taler, 2000

A1
For thirty years
What you gave us was bliss
For thirty years
A caress and a kiss
And all the soul
That you put in our lives
You made the goal
Of a parent so wise

A2
In thirty years
Dreams have grown into life
In thirty years
You became someone's wife
You danced your swings
And amassed your awards
You sounded chords
Which have fluttered gold wings

B (2x)
And now you make
Most people cry
Watching your show
They beautify
Their own life
Their own strife
And then they glow
    (bis)
Like other suns and stars

A1

Laurian Taler

ON A BLADE OF GRASS
Lyrics from my songs

©Laurian Taler, 2014

All rights reserved

Gong Publishing
Toronto

www.gongnog.com

ISBN 978-1-926477-02-2

www.ingramcontent.com/pod-product-compliance
Lightning Source LLC
Chambersburg PA
CBHW070059100426
42743CB00012B/2596